PRAYER BY PRAYER

PRAYER
by
PRAYER

John Eddison

H. E. WALTER LTD

First published in 1983 by
H. E. Walter Ltd
26 Grafton Road, Worthing
West Sussex BN11 1QU, England

© R. J. B. Eddison 1983

ISBN 0 85479 048 9

Acknowledgements to A. R. Mowbray & Co. Ltd.
for prayers from *The Prayer Manual*.

Printed and bound in Great Britain by
The Camelot Press Ltd, Southampton

CONTENTS

Personal Needs

CONTENTS

CONTENTS

FOREWORD

The purpose of this book of Prayers is twofold. First, it is hoped that it will provide a useful collection for those who try to guide the worship of the young in school assemblies, chapels, churches, and on other occasions; and secondly, that it may be of use in the home, and of value at meetings for prayer, or in private times of prayer.

The book has been divided into three main sections. The first is a straightforward collection of ordinary prayers for general use; the second is deliberately designed for much younger children; and the third section is composed of some of the famous prayers which have been used throughout the history of the Christian Church, which are nowadays often unfamiliar, and which have been collected from different sources. The prayers in the first two sections are original, but in section three practically no attempt has been made to modernise the language, or bring the prayers uptodate, because it is felt that if this is necessary at all, it can be done much more satisfactorily by the person who is actually using them. At the very end there is a short 'Litany', based on the familiar framework for all prayers — 'Sorry', 'Thanks' and 'Please'.

Each of the three main sections has itself been divided into three subsections. The first subsection contains prayers which are suitable for special occasions, the seasons of the Church's year, and so on; the prayers in the second subsection are intercessory in nature, and concerned with the needs of others; while those in the third have to do with more personal and individual needs. Each main section has its own list of contents in addition to the full contents list within the preliminary pages. The prayers throughout are arranged in alphabetical order of subject-matter.

Crowborough, Sussex.   John Eddison

August, 1982.

11

Part 1

GENERAL PRAYERS

Contents

15

GENERAL PRAYERS

Special Occasions

ADVENT

We remember at this time, O Lord, how the hearts of people were prepared for your first coming, and how they turned to you, repenting of their sins. We ask you that you will also prepare us for that day when you will return to set up your kingdom upon this earth, and when righteousness and peace will reign for evermore. Help us so to live that we may not be ashamed at your coming, but may gladly welcome you as servants who have done their master's will faithfully and well, through Jesus Christ our Lord.

ASCENSION

Lord, at this time we remember the day when you left this earth and returned to your father's home, there to reign in triumph and glory. Help us sometimes to think of you like that, seated at God's right hand, clothed with majesty and honour, worshipped by all the angels of heaven. You are worthy, O Lord, to receive blessing and honour, glory and power, because of who you are, and because of what you have done for sinful men and women. Hasten the time when every knee shall bow before you, and when the whole world shall acknowledge you to be the one and only controller of the universe, the King of kings and Lord of lords, for your name's sake.

AUTUMN

O Lord, the fading flowers and falling leaves remind us that once more summer is past and over, and though we watch its departure with regret, yet we rejoice in the quiet and sober beauty of autumn. Help us to trace your loving kindness to us not only in the sunshine, but in the shadows, and to remember that sometimes disappointment, trouble and sorrow are but thin disguises of your love, and ways whereby you would bind us more closely to yourself, through Jesus Christ our Lord.

BEGINNING OF TERM

As we stand, O Lord, upon the threshold of a new term, we thank you first of all for the holidays which have just ended, for the happiness of home life, the love of parents and relations, and the pleasures and relaxation of the past weeks. And now we ask for help to settle quickly into the life and work of a new term. May the way we work and play, the thoughtfulness we show to others, and our determination to please you make it happy, successful and memorable for us all, and especially for those who are here for the first time, through Jesus Christ our Lord.

CHRISTMAS

We thank you, O Lord, for Christmas, and for all the excitement and good will which we associate with it. May we not be concerned only with our own desires and pleasures, but keep us mindful of the needs of others, and generous in the use of our money and our time. Above all we ask that we may remember that Christmas was the day on which you came into this world to be the Saviour of mankind. Help us to make time to think of you, amidst all the festivity and the fun; and help us to make room for you at the very centre of our hearts, to reign there as Saviour, Friend and King. We ask it for your own name's sake.

EASTER DAY

O Lord Jesus Christ, we rejoice at this time at your glorious resurrection from the dead. Though you died, you conquered death, and now you are alive for evermore. We thank you that because of this, death is no longer an enemy to be feared, but the gateway to a fuller life. We thank you that Satan is a defeated foe who need have no more dominion over us. We thank you that because you are alive, you are also available, a living companion and friend to all who trust in you. For all this we praise and bless your mighty name, through Jesus Christ our Lord.

EPIPHANY

Lord, we remember that at this time you revealed yourself to the wise men as their long-expected King. Grant that we too, sharing their faith, may worship you as our Saviour and King. Just as you received the gifts of gold and frankincense and myrrh, so accept our gifts O Lord: our time and energy, our hands and hearts. Cleanse them afresh, touch them with your power, and use them to your glory and in your service, through Jesus Christ our Lord.

19

END OF TERM

We thank you O Lord for all the blessings of the past term, and we ask your forgiveness for those occasions when we have disappointed ourselves and others, and have grieved you. We ask for very happy holidays, and that you will help us to contribute to their enjoyment by our own thoughtful and unselfish behaviour at home. Bless those who are leaving this term. Grant them success in their new work, and help them above all things to try to please you and to serve you faithfully all the days of their life, through Jesus Christ our Lord.

❧

EVENING

We thank you, O Lord, for bringing us safely to the end of another day, for protecting us from accident and illness, and for providing us with all our daily needs. We thank you for the gift of sleep, and we ask that you will use it tonight to refresh us in mind and body, and to prepare us for all that tomorrow holds in store. Finally, we commend to you all those who this night will enjoy little or no sleep — those who work while we rest; those who are kept awake through the long hours of darkness by pain, anxiety or sorrow. O Lord, in blessing us, bless them also, and may your peace guard their hearts and minds, through Jesus Christ our Lord.

We commit ourselves and all whom we love into your keeping, O Lord, and ask that you will watch over us during the silent hours of this night, and keep far from us all that might harm us in body or in soul. We thank you for all that has contributed to the happiness of this day: for progress made, for friendship strengthened, for letters received, for success at work or games; and we ask your forgiveness for those times when we have grieved you in thought, word and deed. So bless us tonight, dear Lord, and raise us tomorrow fit and ready to meet all the demands that may be made upon us, through Jesus Christ our Lord.

Forgive us O heavenly Father for all that has made this day less enjoyable than it should have been for ourselves and for others: for times when we have been proud, selfish or lazy; when we have forsaken duty for pleasure; when we have not loved you as we ought. We ask that we may learn by our failures, and that what have been stumbling-blocks today may tomorrow be stepping-stones along our way. Bless us all tonight. Grant us refreshing sleep, and may we rise tomorrow ready to follow you more closely and to serve you better, through Jesus Christ our Lord.

Heavenly Father, we quickly grow tired, but you faint not neither are weary. We need constant rest, but you neither slumber nor sleep. Our eyes grow heavy, but the eyes of the Lord run to and fro throughout the whole earth to watch over His people and to attend to their needs. Therefore, O Lord, give us a steadfast trust in your love and care, and may we go to rest this night in perfect peace, knowing that it is you O Lord only who makes us to dwell in safety, through Jesus Christ our Lord.

EXAMINATIONS

We commend to you, O Lord, all those who at this time are taking examinations, both in this school and elsewhere. Give them the power to remember clearly what they have been taught, to think accurately and to write neatly. May nothing happen to disturb their concentration, and if it be your will grant them good success, through Jesus Christ our Lord.

GOOD FRIDAY

We remember O Lord at this time the great love you showed in dying on the cross to pay the price of sin, and to open the kingdom of heaven to all believers. We thank you for this measureless and undeserved love, and we ask that we may not only enjoy the forgiveness and freedom which you died to purchase, but may also show our gratitude by turning from all we know to be sinful, and serving you faithfully for the rest of our lives, through Jesus Christ our Lord.

∽

LENT

Lord, you have not only taught us that we should discipline our minds and bodies, but in the wilderness you gave us an example of self-control which we should try to follow. Help us to use this season of Lent as an opportunity of making ourselves better and stronger soldiers in your army. Help us to break bad habits which we may have got into, and to form those which will reinforce us in our fight for righteousness. Help us to make good resolutions and to keep them. Help us to realise that it is better to deny ourselves than to gratify every wish. So equip us O Lord to fight more strongly under your banner against the world, the flesh and the devil, through Jesus Christ our Lord.

∽

MATCH OF THE DAY

O Lord, we know that you are interested in everything we do, and we therefore commit to you those who will be playing for the school today. Inspire them with a determination to succeed, playing for each other as well as for themselves. Make them generous in victory, cheerful in defeat, and help them at all times to set a high standard of sportsmanship and fair play, through Jesus Christ our Lord.

MORNING

Heavenly Father, we thank you for the rest of another night, and for bringing us safely to the start of this new day. You can see all that lies ahead of us through the coming hours, and we ask for strength to live them in a way which will be pleasing to you. Give us wisdom always to know which is the right thing to do, and courage and determination to do it. Give us cheerfulness to do what we find dreary or irksome without complaining. Give us patience to tackle the long and difficult task with quiet perseverance. So grant, O Lord, that at evening we may look back upon a day that has been well spent and wisely used, through Jesus Christ our Lord.

Go with us, O Lord, into this unknown day, and help us in all the duties and pleasures which lie ahead. Make us prepared for the unexpected things as well as for those which we know will take place. Keep us watchful against the sudden attack of temptation, that it may not take us unawares. Make us quick to seize every opportunity of helping someone who is in need. Keep us ready for the request we could not foresee and the problem we did not anticipate. So grant, O Lord, that this day may be one in which we prove your help in our lives, and find true happiness in our hearts, through Jesus Christ our Lord.

O Lord, you are the Good Shepherd who goes before his sheep to lead them in the right way, grant that this day we may follow you wherever you shall lead. Go with us into the class-room and on to the playing-field. May we remember your presence in moments of joy or sorrow, of success or failure. Strengthen us when we are tempted, guide us when perplexed, encourage us when we are downhearted or lonely. So, whatever outward things befall us, may this day be lived in the calm of your presence, in the enjoyment of your power, and in the obedience of your will, through Jesus Christ our Lord.

Be with us, O Lord, throughout this day, and help us to do nothing that will spoil it for ourselves or others, or that will bring disappointment or sorrow to you. Make us honest and industrious in our work; generous and thoughtful in our dealings with others; pleasing in everything to you. So grant that no shadow of sin may come between us, and 'at evening may we say we have walked with God today', through Jesus Christ our Lord.

NEW YEAR

We commit into your hands, O Lord, the year which is just beginning. We ask that as far as is good for us we may meet with happiness and success, but especially that we may follow you more faithfully than before. Where we have been weak and yielded too easily to temptation, make us resolute, and determined in your strength to conquer. Where we have been misguided, lead us in the paths of righteousness. Although we cannot see what the future holds and hides, we thank you that you have promised to go with us, and that your presence is better than light, and safer than a known way, through Jesus Christ our Lord.

REMEMBRANCE SUNDAY

We thank you O Lord for the sacrifice of all those who have given their lives for this country, for their devotion to duty, for their courage in battle, and their forgetfulness of self. We pray that we who have inherited the freedom they died to preserve may follow the example they set, and give ourselves more perfectly to the service of our country, the good of our fellow-men and the cause of righteousness and peace, through Jesus Christ our Lord.

SPRING

We see around us O Lord the dawn of nature — buds beginning to break and birds to nest. We thank you for the beauty of these things, and that once again nature is awaking from the long, cold months of sleep. May we too, O Lord, awake to righteousness and bestir ourselves to do your will. Fill us with new energy and new enthusiasm, that we may approach all we have to do in a fresh and lively spirit, through Jesus Christ our Lord.

SUMMER

We thank you dear Lord for the warmth and sunshine of long summer days, for the beauty of the countryside, and for all the sights and sounds of nature. Help us to benefit from these days. May they speak to us of the warmth of your love. Bless those who use them for holidays, for rest and recreation. Bless particularly those who cannot use them in this way: for those whose work binds them to city or factory; for those who labour at night; for those who are handicapped by poverty or sickness. So grant that in our own happiness we may ever be mindful of the needs of others, through Jesus Christ our Lord.

WHITSUNDAY

We remember, O Lord, your last words to the disciples — Lo, I am with you always, even to the end of the world. We thank you that you kept that promise by sending your Holy Spirit to take your place in the hearts of your followers, guiding them into all truth, and abiding with them for ever. Teach us to believe in his unseen presence, and may we do nothing that would grieve him or quench his power. Help us rather to allow him full control, so that he may fill every corner of our hearts with joy and light and love, through Jesus Christ our Lord.

WINTER

We thank you, O Lord, for the seasons of the year, and especially today for the changing moods of winter — for storm and sunshine, wind and rain, frost and ice and snow, for brown fields and bare trees. We thank you too for the comfort and warmth of bed, for food, clothing, companionship and exercise. But we ask for all those who must face the winter months without the benefit of these things: for the disabled and the sick, for the very old and the poor, for the lonely and the unloved. Grant them your help, O Lord, and may we, so far as we are able, to try to relieve them in their need, through Jesus Christ our Lord.

General Requests

CHURCH

O Lord, we ask you to bless your Church, the society of all those who know and love you. Where it is sinful, cleanse it; where it is weak, strengthen it; where it is divided, unite it. Grant, O Lord, that throughout the world its message may be clearly heard, its frontiers extended and its influence increased. Give wisdom, courage and strength to its clergy and ministers, and grant that their example and their teaching may become a shining pathway to the knowledge of your love, through Jesus Christ our Lord.

COMMONWEALTH

We thank you, O Lord, for the Commonwealth, and that so many millions of men and women are united in their loyalty to the Queen and in their love of freedom and justice. Help us to play our part, however small it may be, in making it an increasing force for good in the world. Teach all who belong to it to seek first your kingdom and righteousness, that it may become an instrument for your purpose in the world, and its influence used for the benefit of all mankind, through Jesus Christ our Lord.

∽

COUNTRY

Lord, we thank you that in past days you have blessed our country and made it great. Bless it now, we pray, but help us always to remember that its true greatness in your eyes is not measured by the size of its armies or its material possessions, but by the way in which it respects God and seeks to obey his laws and to walk in his ways. Therefore O Lord, incline our hearts to do your will, through Jesus Christ our Lord.

∽

ENTERTAINMENT AND SPORT

We thank you O Lord for all those to whom you have given the gift of entertaining others, whether on screen or stage, radio or television, or in the field of sport. Help them never to misuse your gift by stooping to unworthy humour or unfair play for the sake of cheap laughter or popularity or for personal gain, but rather to use it for your glory and the good of their fellow-men. And grant too, that we who watch may be refreshed and uplifted by what they do, and return more keenly and readily to our work, through Jesus Christ our Lord.

∽

FARMERS

We pray, O Lord, for all who work on the land, for those who till the soil and tend the cattle, for gardeners, fruit-growers and farmers. We thank you for their devoted work at all times and in all weathers. We ask you to protect them from misfortune and damage, and to prosper their efforts so that in due time we may enjoy the fruit of their labours.

Grant them pride and pleasure in their work, that they may know that in cultivating the earth they are fulfilling your command and helping to meet the needs of mankind. Finally, O Lord, give us thankful hearts, and make us grateful for all that we receive from you as a result of their labour and skill, through Jesus Christ our Lord.

✍

FRIENDS

We commit into your protection, O Lord, our friends and all who are dear to us. Make us always grateful for the happiness and companionship which they bring into our lives. Help us never to fail or disappoint them, but at all times may they be able to count upon our loyalty and sympathy. Above all we ask you that our friendships may be deepened and enriched through our knowledge of the perfect friend, our Saviour Jesus Christ.

✍

HOLIDAY-MAKERS

We commend to you, O Lord, all those who at this time are seeking the rest and recreation of a holiday, and especially any who are known to us. Grant them, if it be your will, fine weather, and freedom from accident or illness. And grant too that in their enjoyment they may not forget you, the giver of all good gifts, through Jesus Christ our Lord.

✍

HOLIDAY TRAVELLERS

Take into your safe keeping, O Lord, all those who will shortly be travelling on their holidays by air. Remove from them any doubt or uncertainty or anxiety about their journeys. Bless and guide those who are responsible for their welfare. Grant them a smooth and uneventful flight, free from storms and interference of any kind; and unite them safely and happily with those they love, through Jesus Christ our Lord.

❧

HOME

We thank you O Lord for the security and happiness of home, for the love of parents and the companionship of relations and friends. May the love that unites us grow deeper with the years, and remain unspoiled by selfishness, ingratitude or pride. May a thoughtful, generous spirit blossom amongst us, nourished by the love we have for you, and by our desire to please you in everything we do, through Jesus Christ our Lord.

We ask you, O Lord, to bless our parents, and to take them this day into your safe keeping. Guard them in time of danger, guide them in difficulty, protect them in temptation. Help us to try to repay their love and generosity by our thoughtfulness for their needs, by the things we do for them, and by the letters we write. So grant that even when we are absent from them, our mutual love and understanding may flourish and increase, and that when the time comes, we may be reunited more deeply and happily than before, through Jesus Christ our Lord.

❧

INDUSTRY

We commit to you, O Lord, all those who are engaged in industry, in the board-room, in the offices and on the shop-floor. Remove all misunderstanding, injustice and prejudice and everything than can damage relationships between one man and another, between management and worker, employer and employee; and may sympathy, good will and fair play prevail. Help those whose work is dreary and monotonous to find contentment and a sense of purpose in what they do, and grant that we may always respect and honour those upon whose skill and industry depend the welfare and prosperity of our country, through Jesus Christ our Lord.

∾

MEDICAL PROFESSION

We thank you, O Lord, for all those whom you have called to be doctors and nurses, and to whom you have given medical skill and sympathy for the sick and the injured. Strengthen and help them in all they have to do. Refresh and restore them when they are over-tired. Guide them when they are perplexed. And grant that they may always look to you, the Good Physician, for the inspiration they need, and as the perfect example of patience, sympathy and care, through Jesus Christ our Lord.

∾

MISSIONARIES

Remember, O Lord, all those who have devoted their lives to your service in other lands. Give them courage and patience, and prosper their work amongst all those who do not know you. Grant, O Lord, that we too may see the urgency of spreading your gospel throughout the world. Inspire us to support missionary work by our prayers, our interest, our gifts, our deeds, and so help us to play our part in bringing the good news of Jesus Christ to all mankind, for his name's sake.

OLD PUPILS

Remember, O Lord, all those who were once at this school. Be with them to day wherever they are, and in storm or sunshine, temptation or prosperity, give them your strength and peace. Grant them if it be your will success in their work, and an ever-widening influence for good; but especially we ask that they may serve you faithfully, and manfully fight under your banner until the end of their lives, through Jesus Christ our Lord.

PRIME MINISTER AND PARLIAMENT

Bless our Prime Minister, O Lord, those who bear office under the crown, and all members of parliament, and strengthen them in their great responsibilities. Put far away from them any cheap desire for personal gain or party advantage. Unite them in seeking the safety, honour and welfare of our Queen and country. May they not conduct their debates or reach their decisions relying upon their own, frail, human wisdom, but upon that which comes to all who seek to follow you and to walk in your ways, through Jesus Christ our Lord.

QUEEN AND COUNTRY

O God our Father we ask you to bless our Queen, the Royal Family, and all who bear authority in our land. Give them wisdom, courage and strength for the many important decisions which they have to make, and grant that guided and upheld by you, they may lead the country into paths of righteousness and peace, through Jesus Christ our Lord.

PEACE IN THE WORLD

O Lord Jesus Christ, it must grieve you who were called the Prince of Peace to see men hating and fighting and killing each other. We ask you to teach those of different races and religions to live together in harmony and goodwill. Give to the statesmen of the world the wisdom they need to remove the causes of war, and to put right those injustices and misunderstandings which lead to conflict. So grant that where there is bitterness love may begin to grow, and in place of strife there may be unity and peace, through Jesus Christ our Lord.

RACIAL HARMONY

We commend to your care, O Lord, the many thousands of coloured people who are living in this country, and we ask you to bless the efforts of all those who are working for racial harmony and understanding. We know that all men, whatever the colour of their skin, are equally precious in your sight, and we ask you to remove all suspicion and prejudice from the hearts of men and women. So grant that increasingly people of different colours and creeds may be able to live happily together, and to work at peace with one another in the same office, factory and school, through Jesus Christ our Lord.

ROAD SAFETY

O Lord, we are sad to hear so often of those who are killed and injured on the roads, and we ask you to help all who use them to exercise proper care and attention. Prevent those who want to drive when they are too tired, or not in a fit condition to do so; and restrain all who are tempted to enjoy speed for its own sake, or to behave in a selfish, discourteous or irresponsible manner. Help those who manufacture and maintain motor vehicles, that no carelessness on their part may aggravate this problem. So grant, O Lord, that through the efforts of all, the number of accidents may be reduced, and this great cause for national shame be removed, through Jesus Christ our Lord.

SCHOOLS AND COLLEGES

We commend to you, O Lord, all those who teach in our universities, colleges and schools. Give them a love and reverence for the truths you have revealed, skill in imparting their knowledge to others, and sympathy and understanding for those they teach. Above all help them to remember that the fear of the Lord is the beginning of wisdom, and that the true purpose of all teaching and learning is to see more clearly your handiwork in nature, in art and in the lives of men, through Jesus Christ our Lord.

SCIENCE

We thank you, O Lord, for the wonders of science, and for all that man has been able to learn about himself, about this planet on which we live, and about the universe around us. May these discoveries never make us proud, but deepen our reverence for you, the Creator and Preserver of all things, and strengthen our faith in your love and power. Grant that we may never yield to the temptation to misuse our knowledge for selfish or unworthy purposes, but that it may always be devoted to the benefit of mankind and the glory of your name, through Jesus Christ our Lord.

SUFFERERS – BEREAVEMENT

O Lord, we ask you to comfort all who mourn the death of those whom they love. May they be uplifted by the memory of their affection and example; strengthened by your continual presence and power; encouraged by the knowledge that for those who love you death is not a precipice over which we fall to be seen no more, but a horizon beyond which we pass into a brighter and a fuller life, through Jesus Christ our Lord.

SUFFERERS – GENERAL

We bring before you O Lord all those who are in any way distressed in mind, body or estate. We think of those who are the victims of disasters like fire, famine or flood. We think of all prisoners and captives, and especially those who suffer for their beliefs. We think of all who have suffered the loss of sight or the power of movement, and who cannot share in the fun and activity of life. We ask, O Lord, that in their troubles they may not lose faith in you, but find themselves upheld at all times by your gracious, omnipotent hand, through Jesus Christ our Lord.

SUFFERERS – NATURAL DISASTERS/HOMELESS

Most merciful Father, who has given to us the comfort of an earthly home and the joy of family life, look down upon all the homeless people in the world – the refugees, the exiles, the victims of war, poverty, disaster or unemployment. Help them to commit their cares to you, and stir the hearts of your people everywhere to come generously to their aid. So grant that they may find relief from their sufferings and a way of happiness out of all their afflictions, through Jesus Christ our Lord.

SUFFERERS — SICKNESS

Lord of compassion and power, look mercifully upon all who suffer. Give them quiet minds and a steadfast faith in your love. Strengthen and guide all those who have the care of them — all doctors and nurses — and grant that by their skill illness may be cured and pain relieved, through Jesus Christ our Lord.

SUFFERERS — TEMPTED

O Lord we ask you to help all those who find temptation too strong for them: those whose wills are weak, whose companions are unhelpful, or who lack the guidance of loving parents and the security of a good home. Help us not to judge them, knowing how easily and how often we ourselves are apt to fall, but may we all remember that through the power of him who loves us and can uphold us by his strength, we may be more than conquerors, and can overcome every temptation, through Jesus Christ our Lord.

TRAVELLERS

O eternal Lord God, you who have made the heavens and the earth, we know that the weather is in your hands, and you can rule the raging of the sea. We commend to you therefore all those who travel by land, by water and in the air, especially any who are known to us at this time. Grant that their voyages may be safe to their persons and their property; bring them to the places where they would be; and may they not forget to give you thanks for your protection and your care, through Jesus Christ our Lord.

WORKERS

O God our loving Father we ask you to bless all those who work so that life may run smoothly and pleasantly for us. We pray for those who cook, or clean, or mend. We remember before you those whose work is dull, or difficult, or lonely. Help us never to take for granted what others do for us, and make us generous in our praise and considerate in our demands, through Jesus Christ our Lord.

We pray O God our Father for all those whose work is dangerous, lonely or difficult — for fishermen and firemen, for miners and policemen, for doctors and nurses, and for those who man our lifeboats and lighthouses. We pray for all who labour that we may live, and who toil while we sleep or play. Grant them satisfaction in their work, O Lord, and in what they do for others help them to remember all that you have done for them, through Jesus Christ our Lord.

WRITERS

O heavenly Father, we ask you to bless all those who write what many read or broadcast what others hear and see. Help them to remember what a great influence they have, and grant that they may publish only what is true and honourable, what is just, pure, lovely and of good report, through Jesus Christ our Lord.

Personal Needs

BIBLE

We thank you, O Lord, for the Bible, for the influence it has been all down the years, and for the help it has brought to so many millions of men and women. Grant that we may learn to value it beyond every other earthly possession, and help us to read it regularly, profitably and with understanding. May it be our sword in time of temptation, the mirror in which we see ourselves as we really are, and the bread by which we grow in faith. Above all we ask that it may lead us into a deeper knowledge of you as our Saviour and Friend, and of the way in which you want your followers to live, through Jesus Christ our Lord.

❧

CHEERFULNESS

O Lord, inspire us to be cheerful, and to look whenever possible upon the bright side of life. Knowing that you are always with us, may we learn to be content, whatever our circumstances may be. Drive from us every sullen and gloomy mood. Give us grateful and uncomplaining hearts, and lead us ever forward in the sunshine of your presence, through Jesus Christ our Lord.

❧

COMMITMENT

Lord, we thank you for the love which took you to the cross to die for us, and for the patience with which you stand at the door of our hearts, knocking and waiting to enter. Give us faith and courage to draw back the bolts of doubt and fear, to fling the door widely open, and to welcome you gladly as our Saviour, Friend and King. We know that once upon a time there was no room for you at the inn. May this never be true of us, but grant that the prayer of each of us may be, 'there is room in my heart, Lord Jesus, there is room in my heart for thee'. We ask this for your own name's sake.

37

COURAGE

O Lord Jesus Christ, you inspired your followers with such courage that in your name they resisted temptation, overcame opposition, and attempted things which seemed impossible. Give us, we pray, the same courage that we may choose the hard right instead of the easy wrong, not minding what other people think or say, or whether they laugh; and when we are tempted to waver, may we remember the courage with which you endured the cross and thought nothing of the shame because of the joy you had in doing your Father's will. We ask this for your name's sake.

❧

DEDICATION

Take command, O Lord, we pray of the citadel of our hearts, and reach out into every corner of our lives. Make us strong to resist evil, quick to learn your way, ready to do your will. Help us to love you with all our hearts, and to show our love not only with our lips, but in our lives, by giving up ourselves to your service, and by walking before you in holiness and righteousness all our days, through Jesus Christ our Lord.

❧

ENDURANCE

Lord, we know that some who start to follow you give up after a time, and go back. Grant that we may not fail in this way. Give us courage that we may endure hardness as good soldiers of Jesus Christ. When we stumble, may we not lose heart, but rise again and press forward more strongly. When we are distracted by the pleasures of the world, help us to keep our eyes upon you. When others tempt us from the right path, keep us steadfast on our course. So grant that we may endure to the end as good and faithful servants, through Jesus Christ our Lord.

❧

FAITH

Lord, we ask you to increase our faith. In time of temptation, may we trust you for the strength we need to conquer. When perplexed, may we look to you to guide us aright. When we feel that things are going wrong, and that the world has turned against us, may we remember your promise that all things work together for good to those who love you. So give us that peace and power which flow from you, that we may meet the changing fortunes of life with serene confidence, through Jesus Christ our Lord.

෴

FORGIVENESS

Forgive us, O Lord, we pray for all the times when we have disappointed and grieved you, and done those things of which our conscience is ashamed. Cleanse us from our faults, and when again faced with the same temptation to be selfish, boastful, unkind or impure, give us the will to choose your way and the strength to conquer, through Jesus Christ our Lord.

Cleanse us, most merciful Father, from all unworthy thoughts and deeds, and fill us with your Holy Spirit, that we may do only those things that are pleasing in your sight. We confess with shame that sometimes we pretend to be better than we are; that we are glad when others go wrong; that we are lazy, deceitful and unkind. Forgive us, we pray, for what we have been, and in your strength and love order and control what we shall be, through Jesus Christ our Lord.

෴

HUMILITY

O Lord, you know how easy it is for us to be proud: to forget that all we have is given by you, and to boast of our ability and achievements. When we are tempted in this way, may we remember that you were meek and lowly in heart. May we remember how much you hate the proud and conceited spirit. And may we determine that while others may praise us, it shall never be our own lips, through Jesus Christ our Lord.

LOVE

O Lord, you have commanded us to love one another, and we ask that you will help us to obey this command. You know that we do not find it difficult to love our friends, but help us also to seek the welfare and happiness of those we do not like, even those whom we think of as enemies. May we do nothing to harm them, but rather look for opportunities of showing them kindness. So grant that in due time the barriers between us may be removed, and that we may find ourselves united with them in a spirit of peace and good will, through Jesus Christ our Lord.

PEACE OF MIND

O Lord, you have told us to be anxious for nothing, but to bring all our troubles to you in prayer. Help us not to grow worried over the misfortunes of life — when things seem to go wrong, when we lose some possession, and even when we make mistakes. We ask, not for a careless attitude towards life, but for one that is carefree, because we have a heavenly Father who knows all our needs, who will allow nothing to harm us without his permission, and who wants us to enjoy his perfect peace. All this we ask for Jesus Christ's sake.

PERSEVERANCE

Lord, we remember how completely you finished the work your Father gave you to do, even though it led you to the cross. Give us strength to persevere in the tasks we are given to do. May we resist the temptation to look for short cuts, to skimp what has to be done, to give up because we are tired or find it difficult, or to leave others to finish what we have begun. Help us rather to see every task as something which we are doing for you, and therefore to do it with all our heart and mind, and with a determination to see that it is thoroughly finished, through Jesus Christ our Lord.

PRAYER

Lord, teach us how to pray with our hearts as well as with our lips. Keep our thoughts from wandering, and help us to remember that you are near to us when we pray, and always ready to hear. If our prayers are not always answered in the way we would like, give us grace to accept your will for us, and to remember that you know best. Even when life is busy, and our time is crowded with everyday activities, help us still to make time to turn to you for the strength and guidance we need, through Jesus Christ our Lord.

O Lord, you have commanded us to pray, and have promised to hear our prayers and answer them according to your will. Teach us how to pray, and help us always to make the most of the opportunities we are given. May we use these times to confess our sins to you, and ask your forgiveness; to thank you for all your goodness; and to make requests for others as well as for ourselves, through Jesus Christ our Lord.

❧

TEMPTATION

O Lord, you know how easily and how often we fall into temptation, and how hard we find it not to be proud, untruthful or bad-tempered. Grant us strength to withstand the attacks of the enemy, and help us always to call upon you in the moment of need, through Jesus Christ our Lord.

We thank you, O Lord, that you have promised victory over temptation to all who trust in you. Grant to us, we pray, the joy of conquering our temptations. Through your strength may we subdue the jealous thought, check the angry, untruthful word, and refrain from any action which might bring hurt to others or dishonour to you, through Jesus Christ our Lord.

THANKSGIVING

Heavenly Father, we thank you for all your great goodness towards us. We thank you for the world, and all the good things in it: for the sky above us, and the earth beneath our feet; for the changing seasons, the sunshine and the rain; for our homes, our relations and friends. Help us not to take your goodness for granted, but constantly to give you thanks, not only by what we say, but by the way we try to please you in everything we do, through Jesus Christ our Lord.

Help us, O Lord, to look back gratefully at the end of each day, and to thank you for all that you have done for us: for success at work or games; for something found which we had mislaid; for the encouragement of friends; for news from home. Above all may we remember to thank you for coming into this world to be our Saviour and Friend, and may we find our true happiness in pleasing you and helping others to know and love you, through Jesus Christ our Lord.

∽

TROUBLE

O Lord, in any time of trouble, doubt or difficulty, give us a sure faith in your love and power, that we may not grow discouraged. Help us to remember that all our ways are known to you, that you see the end from the beginning, and that you can be with us just as really in our darkest moods as in our lightest moments. So grant, dear Lord, that trusting in you, we may mount up with wings as eagles, we may run and not grow weary, we may walk and not faint, through Jesus Christ our Lord.

∽

WORSHIP

Forgive, us O Lord, we beseech you, for all our past sins and failures, and help us now to worship you in spirit and in truth. Take from us all wandering thoughts; incline our hearts and minds to do your will; help us to sing your praise with all our hearts and to listen to your word with open ears, through Jesus Christ our Lord.

Part 2

JUNIOR PRAYERS

Contents

JUNIOR PRAYERS

Special Occasions

ADVENT

Lord, it was at this time nearly two thousand years ago, that you were getting ready to come into this world as a little boy. I do want to thank you for leaving your home of light and joy, and coming down here as my Saviour and Friend. I wasn't here to greet you then, Lord, but perhaps I shall be able to welcome you when you come a second time, not as a baby boy, but this time as a mighty King.

ASCENSION

I hate it Lord, when people I love go away, and have to say 'good-bye', and your disciples must have felt very sad when they saw you disappearing into the clouds. But really they should not have been sad, because you promised to send your Holy Spirit to take your place, and to live in their hearts and in mine too; and also you said that one day you would come back again, just as you had gone.

AUTUMN

It makes me rather sad, Lord, when the days get shorter, and the leaves begin to fall, and the birds fly away for the winter. And then I think how tired we would get if the summer went on and on for ever, and what lovely colours the leaves turn before they fall, and how warm and cosy it is at home. And the more I think like that, the more I want to say 'thank you' for the autumn almost as much as for the spring.

BEGINNING OF TERM

Did you have to go to school, Lord? And did you enjoy it? I quite like it, but I never enjoy the first day, and rather wish the holidays could go on for ever. But I know that would be rather silly, and so I do ask you to help me at the start of this term. May I try really hard and do my very best, because I have a feeling that if I do, then I am going to enjoy it very much.

❧

CHRISTMAS

Lord, it has come at last! I just couldn't wait, and have been counting the days till Christmas. And now Lord, just look at the things in this stocking! And did you see that big parcel waiting for me downstairs? But wait a minute. I'm forgetting that it isn't my birthday, but yours. I am sorry Lord that I forgot that. Many happy returns! But what can I give you as a present? These toys wouldn't be much good to you, I am afraid. I know what you would like. You would like my heart, so that you can come and live there, and make it your palace and your royal throne. Please take it, Lord, with love from me.

❧

EASTER

I love surprises Lord, don't you? I'm sure you do, because you gave your disciples a terrific one on Easter Day. They thought you were still dead, but when they got to the tomb they found that it was quite empty, and then you came and met them and talked with them, just as you had done before. How wonderful and exciting! And to think that you never died again, like other people, but that you are alive for evermore — alive today as my Saviour and Friend! Thank you Lord!

❧

END OF TERM

Lord, the holidays have come at last! I thought they never would, but here they are. I wonder whether you looked forward to them as much as I do. I expect so, because you too had a lovely home to go to and lots to do. But I know that you didn't just think about having a good time yourself, but you tried to make other people happy by thinking of them first. Please help me to do the same, so that we can all look back on these holidays as the happiest we have ever had.

✎

EVENING

Thank you, heavenly Father, for all that I have been able to do today: for my lessons and my games; for all the fun I have had and the food; for mum and dad and all my friends. Please forgive me for anything that I have done which has made you or other people sad, and may tomorrow be an even better day. And now, as I go to bed, 'Lord, keep me safe this night, secure from all my fears; protect and guard me while I sleep, till morning light appears'.

✎

GOOD FRIDAY

Lord, this must have been a terrible day for you. I can't bear to think about all the hatred, the shame and the pain you had to suffer. And you did it all for me, that my sins might be forgiven, and that I and others too who put their trust in you might one day go to live with you in heaven. I can't say 'thank you' enough. For 'it is a thing most wonderful, almost too wonderful to be, that God's own Son should come from heaven and die to save a child like me'.

✎

MORNING

Heavenly Father, you know that I don't like getting up very much, but I wouldn't want to spend all day in bed, and there are lots of things I look forward to doing today. May it be a very happy day, not just because I do well at lessons or games, but because I really try to please you in all I do; and because I overcome some of the temptations which beat me yesterday; and because I think of you first, then of other people, and last of all of myself.

NEW YEAR

Do you know Lord, I am rather glad to say good-bye to last year. I enjoyed it all right, but it is rather fun having a brand new one in front of me, like a great field of snow on which no one has yet trodden. But I do ask Lord that when I get to the end of it and look back I may see that my footsteps have kept to a straight path, and haven't wandered off in the wrong direction — as I am afraid they sometimes did last year, into the byeways of selfishness, disobedience and pride.

∽

SPRING

Lord, have you seen the crocuses and the snow drops? I'm sorry, of course you have, because you put them there! But I do love them because they show that the winter is over at last, and soon the daffodils will come, and the birds begin to make their nests. Lord, spring helps me to understand that when people die, they really only go to sleep, like the trees and the flowers, and then wake up again to a new and wonderful life. Thank you Lord for showing me this — that death is not the end, but a new beginning: not a 'terminus' where we stop for ever, but a 'junction' where we change.

∽

SUMMER

I think summer has come at last Lord, and how I love these long sunny days when I don't need a jersey, when the swimming pool is so super, and when I can stay up later and play out of doors. Thank you Lord for all the seasons, but perhaps especially for the summer. In the autumn you seem to sigh, just a little sadly. In the winter you almost frown. In the spring you smile, but now that summer has come I do believe you are laughing, and wanting us to share your enjoyment of this lovely world you have made and everything in it. Thank you, Lord, again.

WHITSUN

Heavenly Father, I'm afraid I don't really understand about the Holy Spirit, but I believe it means that in some way Jesus can be everywhere at once, and it is wonderful to think that I can have him with me just as once he was with Peter, James and John. Help me to remember that he is always with me, even though I can't see him, and may I do nothing to make him sad, or sorry that he is walking with me.

∽

WINTER

I don't look forward to winter, Lord, but when it comes, I do really enjoy it. I can do the indoor things I don't feel like doing in the summer, and I love the holly and the fires and the frost and Christmas; and I don't mind going to bed so much. But for some people who can't run about as I can it must be a cold and difficult time, and I ask you to help them and to keep them safe.

∽

General Requests

ANIMALS

Lord, what would we do without animals! How dull life would be! And we do thank you for making so many different kinds: the tame ones, like cats and dogs which we keep as pets, and which become our friends, and the wild ones which run away when they see us, but only because they are afraid we might hurt them. May we always remember that you made them all, just as you made us, and help us never to be cruel towards them, but always kind and gentle.

BIBLE

Heavenly Father, thank you for all my books, but above all for the Bible. I am afraid I don't always understand what I read, but I thank you for the parts that I do understand, and specially for those that tell me about the coming of Jesus, and his great love in dying on the cross for me. May I learn to love the Bible more and more, and try to read it every day.

BIRDS

Lord, what fun the birds are! I do thank you for making so many. I thank you for the cheeky ones, like the robins and the sparrows. I thank you for those I can hear singing like the thrush and the blackbird and for those I hear sometimes at night when I lie awake, and for those I only just see once in a while. Thank you Lord that they bring so much happiness and music into our lives, and help me to be always like them — cheerful and carefree.

BOOKS

Thank you Lord for all the books on my shelves at home. Help me to treasure them, to read them and to try and understand them. And I ask you to help all those who are good at telling stories, that they may write what is beautiful and true, so that all who read may come to know more about this wonderful world in which we live, and about your great love.

CHURCH

Thank you Lord for my church. You know how sometimes I really love going, and sometimes I find it a bit boring. If this is my fault, Lord, please forgive me, and may I try harder to enjoy it and to mean all that I say. Help all the people who look after the church: the ministers, and those who clean it and decorate it; and make me one of its loyal and happy members.

DOCTORS AND NURSES

Heavenly Father, I don't often have to see the doctor, but when I do, I thank you that he is so kind and careful; and to day I pray for all doctors and nurses. When a lot of people are all ill at once, they must be very busy and get very tired, and I ask you to help them in everything they have to do. May they remember that you too were a doctor, who went about healing people, and may they trust you to make them wise and patient and kind.

FACTORY WORKERS

I pray today Lord for all those men and women who work in factories, and specially for those who can't really enjoy what they are doing, because their work is boring, and yet we cannot get on without it. Help them to try to remember that even the dullest task can be made brighter and more interesting if we do it, not just to please ourselves, but to try to please you.

FARMERS

Heavenly Father, what a lot we owe to the farmers in our country! All the year round, in sunshine and rain, in frost and fog, they have to tend the crops and care for the animals. Make me grateful for all their hard work, and may it bring joy to them to know that the earth belongs to you, and that in looking after it they are not only helping to feed people, but obeying the first command you ever gave.

FLOWERS

I thank you for the flowers — for the wild ones we find when we are out for a walk, and also for those we can grow in the garden and keep in the house. I thank you for the brave ones that come out when it is still winter, and for the bright ones which make us feel cheerful and glad. Especially we ask that today they may bring joy to people who are lonely, sad, or sick, and remind them of your beauty and your love.

FRIENDS

Father, we thank you for our friends — those we make at school and at home. We thank you for all they do to make us happy, and that we can talk with them, laugh and play with them. Help us never to lose a good friend by being unkind or untruthful, and to remember how good you are to your friends, even when they hurt you and sadden you by what they say and do.

GAMES

Heavenly Father, you know how much I love games: indoor games by the fire, but even more, games I can play out of doors like football and cricket. Thank you for allowing them to be invented. Help me always to try hard and to play keenly, but may I never be selfish or unfair. When I win, Lord, may I not become proud, and when I lose, help me never to grumble or complain.

HANDICAPPED PEOPLE

Lord, I thank you that I can see and hear, walk and run and jump; but there are thousands of boys and girls who can't do these things, because they are sick, or crippled or handicapped in some way. Make me specially helpful and kind to any I know or meet. Help them to be brave and cheerful, in spite of all the things they can't do; and guide and strengthen all those who take care of them, and who try to make their lives easy and happy.

HARVEST

Lord, I saw them today just beginning to bring in the harvest. Please grant that they may have sunny weather to do this and that it may be a good one; and give all who work in the fields special strength at this time. And thank you Lord for once more keeping your promise to supply us with our daily bread.

HOMES, CLOTHING, FOOD

Heavenly Father, there are some things I enjoy every day and I am afraid I often forget to thank you for them. So today I want to thank you for the house I live in, for the skill of those who built it, and for those who keep it nice and clean. Thank you too for the clothes I wear, and for those who made them and bought them for me. And then thank you for the food I eat, and for those who provide and prepare it. Help me to remember that all these good gifts really come from you, so thank you again, Lord.

❧

MINISTERS AND CLERGY

Lord, I thank you for all clergymen and ministers who are trying to spread the good news about Jesus to other people. It can't always be an easy thing to do, because some people don't want to listen and some never go to church; but please help and encourage them, and may they be able to bring many people to know and to love you.

❧

MISSIONARIES

Thank you Lord that many years ago Christians from other countries came to tell people in Great Britain about Jesus Christ and his love. Thank you for their faith and their courage. And now I pray for all those who have gone out from this country into other lands with the same message to try to help people who have never heard of you. Be with them when they feel lonely or perhaps afraid. Give them good success in their work, and may many others come to love you because of what they do.

❧

MUSIC

Heavenly Father, I love singing, and I do thank you for inventing music. Thank you for giving some people such lovely voices, and helping others to play so many different instruments. May what I sing and what I hear always help to make me and other people happy, and to think of your beauty and your love.

PARLIAMENT

Heavenly Father, I don't really understand very much about the government and parliament and all that goes on there; but I do know that just as dad has to look after our home, so people have to look after this country, and this means making good rules and spending the money wisely. So I ask you Lord to help all those who govern us to do the right things. May they always try to please you and do what you would like; and may they always care for the safety and welfare of the people you entrust to them.

༄

PARENTS AND RELATIONS

Thank you Lord for my parents, for my brothers and sisters and for all my other relations. May I do all I can to make our family a really happy one. Help me not to be selfish, and always wanting my own way. Make me a really nice person to have at home, and show me ways in which I can help mum and dad by being thoughtful, kind and obedient.

༄

POLICE, FIREMEN, MINERS, SEAMEN, etc.

Lord, what about policemen and firemen, miners and seamen, and others whose work is hard and dangerous? I so easily forget them, but I do ask you that you won't do so, because they need your help and presence Lord, especially when they are in difficulty or danger. Give them courage, and help them not to be afraid; and show me if there are little ways in which I can help to bring more happiness into their lives.

༄

PUBLIC SERVANTS, POSTMEN, etc.

Lord, where would we be without those people who call at our houses almost every day! The postman, the milkman, the dustmen. And then there are the traffic wardens, the lolly-pop men, the bus drivers and so many others! Thank you Lord, because they do so much for us that we could not do for ourselves. Help them always to be cheerful and content, even though their work is sometimes dull and difficult, and the weather is horrid, and their pay perhaps not very good.

THE QUEEN AND THE ROYAL FAMILY

Lord, what a super person the Queen is! I do thank you for her and for her family. I thank you for the example they set. I thank you for the care and interest they take in all of us. Give them great happiness in their work — a happiness which comes from knowing that we love them, but most of all that you love them too.

∽

RACE RELATIONS

Lord, I know it doesn't matter to you what colour a person's skin is, and you must hate it when you see one person being cruel to another because one is black and the other white, or perhaps the other way round. Help me always to think of everyone, whatever their colour, as people you have made, and whom you loved and came to save; and may this thought stop me at once if ever I feel like being unkind or unfriendly towards anyone of another race.

∽

ROAD SAFETY

Lord, it is awful — the number of people who are killed and injured in road accidents; and it need not happen if only people were careful and sensible. Do make all who use the roads wise and thoughtful. Help them not to get impatient when they can't overtake a lorry, or angry when someone else makes a mistake, or want to show off how fast they can drive. And may I do my part too by keeping all the rules that people have made for our safety.

∽

SAILORS, SOLDIERS AND AIRMEN

Heavenly Father, we thank you today for all those who defend our country — for all soldiers, sailors and airmen. We thank you for what they have done in the past to protect and guard us, and we thank you too for all those who have died fighting to keep this country safe. We ask you to be with them each day, especially those in places of danger, and to make them brave and strong in the many difficult things which they have to do.

SCHOOL

Lord, sometimes I wish I didn't have to go to school, and that it could always be holidays, and then I think how silly that would be, and how sad to grow up without learning so many useful things. And so I thank you for school and for those who try to teach me, and I ask that they may really enjoy doing so, because they see that I like my lessons, and want to learn, and to grow up wise and sensible.

❧

SCIENTISTS, EXPLORERS, INVENTORS

Heavenly Father, I want to thank you today for all scientists, explorers and inventors. You want us to understand the world in which we live, and so we ask you to guide all those who are trying to help us to do so by discovering its secrets and unfolding its mysteries. Give them great wisdom, and grant that what they find out may not only be a help to all mankind and be wisely used, but may also teach them to know you better and to love you more.

❧

SHOPKEEPERS

Lord, what a busy time shopkeepers must have! On their feet all day long, and having to deal with all kinds of people: those who are always in a hurry, those who can't make up their minds, those who grumble and even those who are rude. Help them Lord to be bright and patient and cheerful, and whenever I go into a shop may I be as kind and as thoughtful as I possibly can.

❧

SICK AND SUFFERING

I feel so sorry, Lord, for people who are ill and lonely and sad, or who are too old to move about very much, and do all the things that they would like to do, and used to do when they were my age. I ask you to help and comfort people like that, and especially any whom I know and can think of now. Show me, Lord, if there is anything I can do to help them: an errand I can run, a message I can take, or a visit I can pay, or anything else that would bring light and perhaps laughter into their lives.

SPORTSMEN

I pray today Lord for all sportsmen, for cricketers and footballers, for runners and swimmers and for all others. I thank you that watching them gives me so much pleasure. Help them not to be proud when they do well, or to feel too sad when they fail. May they always be fair to each other and remember to set a good example to the millions who watch and admire them. And may they never forget to be thankful to you for giving them such skill and strength.

◈

TEACHERS

Today, Lord, I want to thank you for all those who teach me. I am afraid sometimes I am rather lazy and stupid, and sometimes I do not even attend. I am sorry Lord, and I ask that I may show how grateful I am to them by really trying to do my best; and I ask you to help all who try to teach me, and to give them patience and wisdom.

◈

TELEVISION

Lord, you know how I love watching television, and I do thank you for it, and for the pleasure it gives. I pray for all those producers and actors who amuse me, or teach me, or thrill me. May what they say and do never disappoint you. Help me not to watch programmes that you wouldn't like to sit beside me and see, and help me not to watch at all when I really ought to be doing something else.

◈

TRAVELLERS

Heavenly Father, I wonder how many people are travelling at this moment. You must know, but I can only guess; and it must be millions — in trains and cars, in the air and on the sea. I ask especially for any who are in difficulty or danger, and any who are known to me. Keep them safe, and bring them where they want to be. Give to all pilots, drivers and helmsmen wisdom and skill, and may they learn to trust you to help them in the difficult work they have to do.

TREES

Thank you Lord for the trees: those that seem to die in the autumn and then come alive again in the spring; and for those that are green all the year round. I love to see the sun shining on their bark, the rain glistening on their leaves, and the wind complaining in their branches. As I look at them, Lord, may they whisper to me and remind me of your power and of your peace.

WEATHER

When I think about the weather Lord, I do want to thank you that it isn't always the same. I thank you for the hot, sunny days; for the wild and windy ones; for snow and rain and ice; and, yes, just sometimes, Lord, for mists and fogs. How boring it would be if every day were the same, and so I thank you Lord for making it all different, and if sometimes it isn't exactly what I want, help me not to grumble, but to remember that you know best.

Personal Needs

CHEERFULNESS

Lord, help me always to be bright and cheerful, even when things are not always quite as I would like them to be. Make me quick to smile, ready to laugh. May my school and my home be a happier, sunnier place because I am there, and may other people be glad to have me around because I help to brighten their lives.

FORGIVENESS

Heavenly Father, I am afraid I don't have to think very hard before I can remember wrong things that I have said and done and even thought. Thank you for dying on the cross to put away my sins. Please forgive me now, and if I have hurt other people as well as you, help me to tell them too that I am sorry. And please help me not to fall into the same temptation again.

KINDNESS

Lord, people are so kind to me, even when I don't deserve it. They look after me, give me things and feed and clothe me. Thank you so much for all they do. And yet sometimes I am not as kind to other people as I should be. I am often cross and selfish. Please help me to try very hard to think kind thoughts about people, and then I know that my words will be kind too, and my deeds as well.

∾

LOVE

I find it quite easy, Lord, in my heart to love my parents and friends, and many of my relations, but may I remember that 'the love in my heart wasn't put there to stay, for it isn't real love till I give it away'. So please help me, Lord, to show the love that I feel by the kind and generous things that I do. And I ask too that I may try very hard to act in this way towards people whom I don't like very much; and perhaps in doing so I shall come to like them better.

∾

OBEDIENCE

Lord, I read in the Bible that you were obedient to your parents. Did you find it difficult sometimes? Because I do. So please help me to be like you, even when I don't like what they ask me to do, and even when I don't see why I should do it. Help me to remember that it is by obeying them like this that I can show just how much I love them.

∾

PRAYER

Heavenly Father, you have told us that we ought to pray, but I am afraid I don't always find it easy. Sometimes I don't want to pray very much, and sometimes when I start my mind wanders on to all sorts of other things. Please help me when I pray to think of you, and that you are beside me like a friend, wanting me to tell you as simply as I can everything about myself and the things that I do.

SERVICE

Lord, when you were down on this earth you always seemed to be going about doing good to people, helping them and healing them, even though they sometimes forgot to say 'thank you'. Please help me to be like that, and each day may I try to find something I can do that will help those who are in difficulty, cheer up those who may be feeling sad or lonely, and make everyone I meet just a little bit happier.

∽

TEMPTATION

Sometimes, Lord, I find it very easy to do bad things and very hard to be good, and I am afraid Satan is often too strong for me. I ask Lord that when those times come, I may feel you to be specially near, and that you will fight Satan for me, and tell him from me that I don't want to be untruthful or unkind, selfish or proud.

∽

THANKFULNESS

Lord, I do hate it when people don't say 'thank you' when I do something for them, and yet I am afraid I often forget to say 'thank you' to you, and it must make you feel very sad sometimes. So today I want to thank you Lord for all you have done for me: for life and health, for happiness and laughter and fun; for my family and friends, my home and food — for everything; but especially I want to thank you for coming into this world to be my Saviour and Friend — for dying on the cross to forgive my sins, and then for rising again to be with me for evermore.

∽

TROUBLE

Lord, do you know that horrid feeling when something has gone wrong? You don't feel very well, or you've lost something, or lessons aren't going well, or you lose a game?

Well, that's how I feel today! I don't quite see how I can put things right, not all at once anyway, but you have promised to be with me in the 'valleys' as well as on the 'mountain tops', and so I ask you to be specially close to me today and to help me.

❧

UNSELFISHNESS

Did you always find it easy Lord to think of others before yourself? Because I'm afraid I don't. I do rather like having my own way, and getting the biggest and the best for myself. But I know really how wrong this is, and how unlike you, and so I ask you to help me not to be selfish. May I learn not always to push myself forward, but to try to say 'after you' instead of 'me first'.

❧

WORSHIP

Heavenly Father, you have promised to be my friend, but may I never forget that you are also my King. When I think of you and when I talk to you in my prayers, may I picture someone who is always at hand to help, and yet also someone who reigns in heaven as a King — the great and almighty maker of this universe.

Part 3

GREAT PRAYERS FROM THE PAST

Contents

GREAT PRAYERS FROM THE PAST

Special Occasions

ADVENT

Almighty God, give us grace that we may cast away the works of darkness, and put upon us the armour of light, now in the time of this mortal life, in which thy Son Jesus Christ came to visit us in great humility; that in the last day, when he shall come again in his glorious majesty, to judge both the living and the dead, we may rise to the life immortal; through him who liveth and reigneth with thee and the Holy Ghost, now and ever.

Prayer Book 1662

ALL SAINTS

Almighty and everlasting God, who dost kindle the flame of thy love in the hearts of thy saints; grant to our minds the same faith and power of love; that as we rejoice in their triumph, we may also follow the example of their patience; through Jesus Christ our Lord.

Gothic Missal

Almighty God, who dost choose thine elect out of every nation, and dost show forth thy glory in their lives: grant, we pray thee, that following the example of thy saints, we may be fruitful in good works to the praise of thy holy name; through Jesus Christ our Lord.

Scottish Prayer Book

ASCENSIONTIDE

Almighty God, whose blessed Son, our Saviour Jesus Christ, ascended far above all heavens that he might fill all things: mercifully give us faith to perceive that according to his promise he abideth with his church on earth, even unto the end of the world; through the same Jesus Christ our Lord.

Scottish Prayer Book

Grant, we beseech thee, almighty God, that like as we do believe thy only-begotten Son our Lord Jesus Christ to have ascended into the heavens; so we may also in heart and mind thither ascend, and with him continually dwell, who liveth and reigneth with thee and the Holy Ghost, one God, world without end.

Prayer Book, 1662

O God the king of glory, who hast exalted thine only Son Jesus Christ with great triumph unto thy kingdom in heaven: we beseech thee leave us not comfortless; but send to us thine Holy Ghost to comfort us, and exalt us unto the same place whither our Saviour Christ is gone before, who liveth and reigneth with thee and the Holy Ghost, one God, world without end.

Prayer Book, 1662

ASH WEDNESDAY AND LENT

Almighty and everlasting God, who hatest nothing that thou hast made, and dost forgive the sins of all them that are penitent: create and make in us new and contrite hearts, that we worthily lamenting our sins, and acknowledging our wretchedness, may obtain of thee, the God of all mercy, perfect remission and forgiveness; through Jesus Christ our Lord.

Prayer Book, 1662

CHRISTMAS

O God, whose blessed Son Jesus Christ became man that we might become the sons of God: grant, we beseech thee, that being made partakers of the divine nature of thy Son, we may be conformed to his likeness; who liveth and reigneth with thee and the Holy Ghost, now and ever.

Scottish Prayer Book

O God, who makest us glad with the yearly remembrance of the birth of thine only Son Jesus Christ: grant, that as we joyfully receive him as our Redeemer, so we may with sure confidence behold him, when he shall come to be our Judge; who liveth and reigneth with thee and the Holy Spirit, one God, world without end.

Gelasian Sacramentary

Almighty God, who hast given us thy only-begotten Son to take our nature upon him, and as at this time to be born of a pure virgin; grant that we being regenerate, and made thy children by adoption and grace, may daily be renewed by thy Holy Spirit; through the same our Lord Jesus Christ, who liveth and reigneth with thee and the same Spirit, ever one God, world without end.

Prayer Book, 1662

CONFIRMATION

O God, who through the teaching of thy Son Jesus Christ didst prepare the disciples for the coming of the Comforter: make ready, we beseech thee, the hearts and minds of thy servants who at this time are seeking the gift of the Holy Spirit through the laying on of hands, that, drawing near with penitent and faithful hearts, they may be filled with the power of his divine indwelling; through the same Jesus Christ our Lord.

Prayer Book, 1928

EASTERTIDE

O God, who through thine only-begotten Son Jesus Christ hast overcome death and opened unto us the gate of everlasting life: grant that, as he was raised from the dead by the glory of the Father, so we may walk in newness of life, and seek those things which are above; where with thee, O Father, and the Holy Spirit, he liveth and reigneth for ever and ever.

The Prayer Manual, 1951

Almighty God, who through thine only-begotten Son Jesus Christ hast overcome death, and opened unto us the gate of everlasting life: we humbly beseech thee, that as by thy special grace preventing us thou dost put into our minds good desires, so by thy continual help we may bring the same to good effect; through Jesus Christ our Lord, who liveth and reigneth with thee and the Holy Ghost, ever one God, world without end.

Prayer Book, 1662

END OF THE YEAR

Almighty God, who alone art without variableness or shadow of turning, and hast safely brought us through the changes of time to the beginning of another year: we beseech thee to pardon the sins that we have committed in the year which is past; and give us grace that we may spend the remainder of our days to thy honour and glory; through Jesus Christ our Lord.

Church of Ireland Prayer Book

EPIPHANY

O God, who by the leading of a star didst manifest thy only-begotten Son to the Gentiles: mercifully grant, that we, who know thee now by faith, may after this life have the fruition of thy glorious Godhead; through Jesus Christ our Lord.

Prayer Book, 1662

O Father everlasting, the light of faithful souls, who didst bring the nations to thy light and kings to the brightness of thy rising: fill the world with thy glory, we beseech thee, and show thyself unto all the nations; through him who is the true light and the bright and morning star, Jesus Christ, thy Son our Lord.

Gothic Missal

❧

EVENING

Look down, O Lord, from thy heavenly throne, and illuminate the darkness of this night with thy celestial brightness, and from the sons of light banish the deed of darkness; through Jesus Christ our Lord.

Office of Compline

O Lord, support us all the day long of this troublous life, until the shades lengthen and the evening comes, and the busy world is hushed, the fever of life is over, and our work done. Then, Lord, in thy mercy grant us safe lodging, and holy rest, and peace at the last; through Jesus Christ our Lord.

Anon.

Lighten our darkness, we beseech thee, O Lord; and by thy great mercy defend us from all perils and dangers of this night; for the love of thy only Son, our Saviour Jesus Christ.

Prayer Book, 1662

❧

GOOD FRIDAY

Grant, O Lord, that in thy wounds I may find my safety, in thy stripes my cure, in thy pain my peace, in thy cross my victory, in thy resurrection my triumph, and a crown of righteousness in thy glorious kingdom.

Jeremy Taylor

Almighty and everlasting God, who of thy tender love towards mankind hast sent thy Son, our Saviour Jesus Christ, to take upon him our flesh and to suffer death upon the cross, that all mankind should follow the example of his great humility; mercifully grant that we may both follow the example of his patience, and also be made partakers of his resurrection; through the same Jesus Christ our Lord.

Prayer Book, 1662

HARVEST-TIDE

Almighty Father, Lord of heaven and earth; of thy great goodness, we beseech thee to give and preserve to our use the kindly fruits of the earth, the treasures of mines, and the harvest of the sea, so as in due time we may enjoy them with thanksgiving.

Archibishop Benson

O almighty and everlasting God, who hast given unto us the fruits of the earth in their season, and hast crowned the year with thy goodness: give us grateful hearts, that we may unfeignedly thank thee for all thy loving-kindness, and worthily magnify thy holy name; through Jesus Christ our Lord.

Bishop John Dowden

HOLY COMMUNION

O Lord, who in a wonderful sacrament didst leave us a memorial of thy cross and passion: grant us so to venerate the sacred mysteries of thy body and blood, that we may always perceive within ourselves the fruits of thy redemption; who livest and reignest with the Father and the Holy Spirit, one God, world without end.

Thomas Aquinas.

MORNING

O God, who dividest day from night, give us hearts and minds unshadowed by the gloom of evil; that we may think continually upon things that are good and wholesome, and be always pleasing in thy sight, through Jesus Christ our Lord.

Gelasian Sacramentary

Into thy hands, O Lord, we commend ourselves and all who are dear to us this day. Be with us in our going out and in our coming in. Strengthen us for the work which thou hast given us to do. And grant that, filled with thy Holy Spirit, we may walk worthy of our high calling, and cheerfully accomplish those things that thou wouldest have done; through Jesus Christ our Lord.

Bishop Theodore Woods

O Lord our heavenly Father, almighty and everlasting God, who hast safely brought us to the beginning of this day: defend us in the same with thy mighty power; and grant that this day we fall into no sin, neither run into any kind of danger; but that all our doings may be ordered by thy governance, to do always what is righteous in thy sight; through Jesus Christ our Lord.

Prayer Book, 1662

The day returns and brings us the petty round of irritating concerns and duties. Help us to play the man, help us to perform them with laughter and kind faces, let cheerfulness abound with industry. Give us to go blithely on our business all day, bring us to our resting beds weary and content and undishonoured, and grant us in the end the gift of sleep.

R. L. Stevenson

~

WHITSUNDAY

O almighty God, who on the day of Pentecost didst send the Holy Ghost the Comforter to abide in thy church unto the end: bestow upon us and upon all thy faithful people his manifold gifts of grace, that with minds enlightened by his truth, and hearts purified by his presence, we may day by day be strengthened with power in the inner man; through Jesus Christ our Lord, who with thee and the same Spirit liveth and reigneth, one God, world without end.

Bishop John Dowden

God, who as at this time didst teach the hearts of thy faithful people, by sending to them the light of thy Holy Spirit: grant us by the same Spirit to have a right judgement in all things, and evermore to rejoice in his holy comfort; through the merits of Christ Jesus our Saviour, who liveth and reigneth with thee, in the unity of the same Spirit, one God, world without end.

Prayer Book, 1662

For Others

CHILDREN

Almighty God and heavenly Father, we thank thee for the children whom thou hast given to us; give us also grace to train them in thy faith, fear and love; that as they advance in years they may grow in grace, and be found hereafter in the number of thine elect children; through Jesus Christ our Lord.

Bishop Cosin.

CHURCH, CHURCH WORKERS, etc.

Gracious Father, we humbly beseech thee, for thy holy catholic church; fill it with all truth, and with all peace. Where it is corrupt, purge it; where it is in error, direct it; where it is superstitious, rectify it; where anything is amiss, reform it; where it is right, strengthen and confirm it; where it is in want, furnish it; where it is divided and rent asunder, make up the breaches of it; O thou holy one of Israel.

Archibishop Laud

Almighty God, grant we beseech thee, to all whom thou has called to the sacred ministry of thy church, such a sense of their high calling that they may count no sacrifice too great to make in thy service; and that so, bringing a blessing to their people, they may themselves be blessed of thee; for the sake of Jesus Christ our Lord.

Canon Peter Green.

Almighty and everlasting God, who alone workest great marvels: send down upon our bishops and clergy, and all congregations committed to their charge, the healthful Spirit of thy grace; and that they may truly please thee, pour upon them the continual dew of thy blessing. Grant this, O Lord, for the honour of our advocate and mediator, Jesus Christ.

Prayer Book, 1662

O thou true light that lightest every man, coming into the world: we pray thee in thy mercy to inflame the heart and enlighten the understanding of all whom thou dost call to the service of thy church; that they may cheerfully acknowledge and readily obey thy call, to the benefit of thy people and the glory of thy holy name; who with the Father and the Holy Spirit livest and reignest, world without end.

Canon H. P. Liddon.

∽

FRIENDS

O almighty and eternal God, through whose providence men are bound together by the ties of blood and holy affection: pour down upon our relations and friends the manifold gifts of thy grace; that, united in faith and love, we may labour together according to thy will for the establishment of thy kingdom; through Jesus Christ our Lord.

Bishop Westcott.

Be pleased, O Lord, to remember my friends, all that have prayed for me, and all that have done me good. Do thou good to them, and return all their kindness double into their own bosom, rewarding them with blessings, sanctifying them with thy grace, and bringing them at last to thy glory.

After Jeremy Taylor.

༄

HOMES AND FAMILIES

Almighty God, from whom every family in heaven and on earth is named: we entreat thy mercy for the families of this and every land, for man and wife and child, and for all who have the care of children; that by thy hallowing our homes may be blessed and our children may grow up in the knowledge of thee and of thy Son, Jesus Christ our Lord.

St. Paul's Cathedral.

Be present with us, O Lord, in our daily duties, and grant to those who dwell in this house the strength and protection of thy continual help; that thou mayest be known as the master of the family and the defender of this home; through Jesus Christ our Lord.

After Gelasian Sacramentary

༄

MISSIONS

O God, who hast made of one blood all nations of men for to dwell on the face of the earth, and didst send thy blessed Son, Jesus Christ, to preach peace to them that are afar off, and to them that are nigh; grant that all the peoples of the world may feel after thee and find thee; and hasten, O heavenly Father, the fulfilment of thy promise to pour out thy spirit upon all flesh; through Jesus Christ our Lord.

Bishop Cotton.

O God, our heavenly Father, who didst manifest thy love by sending thine only-begotten Son into the world that all might live through him: pour thy Spirit upon thy church that it may fulfil his command to preach the gospel to every creature; send forth, we beseech thee, labourers into thy harvest; defend them in all dangers and temptations; and hasten the time when the fulness of the Gentiles shall be gathered in, and all Israel shall be saved; through the same thy Son, Jesus Christ our Lord.

Prayer Book, 1928

〜

NEEDY PEOPLE

O God, the God of all righteousness, mercy, and love, give us grace and strength to conceive and execute whatever may be for thine honour and the welfare of the needy; that we may become at last, through the merits and intercession of our common Redeemer, a great and happy because a wise and understanding people.

The 7th Earl of Shaftesbury

Almighty God, Father of all mercies and giver of all comfort; deal graciously, we pray thee, with those who mourn, that casting every care on thee, they may know the consolation of thy love; through Jesus Christ our Lord.

Prayer Book, 1928

We humbly beseech thee, of thy goodness, O Lord, to comfort and succour all them who in this transitory life are in trouble, sorrow, need, sickness, or any other adversity: help us to minister to them thy strength and consolation, and so endow us with the grace of sympathy and compassion that we may bring to them both help and healing; through Jesus Christ our Lord.

Prayer Book, 1549

Watch thou, O Lord, with those who wake, or watch, or weep tonight, and give thine angels charge over those who sleep. Tend thy sick ones, O Lord, Christ; rest thy weary ones; bless thy dying ones; soothe thy suffering ones; pity thine afflicted ones; shield thy joyous ones. And all for thy love's sake.

St. Augustine

Remember every Christian soul, afflicted and oppressed, and struggling and needing thy mercy and succour; and our brethren that are in captivity and in prisons and bonds and bitter thraldoms: supplying return to the wanderers, health to the sick, deliverance to the captives, and rest to them that have fallen asleep aforetime.

Lancelot Andrewes

❧

ROYAL FAMILY

Almighty God, the fountain of all goodness: give ear, we beseech thee, to our prayers, and multiply thy blessings upon thy servant, Elizabeth our Queen; defend her evermore from all dangers, ghostly and bodily; make her a great example of virtue and piety, and a blessing to this kingdom; through Jesus Christ our Lord, who liveth and reigneth with thee, O Father, in the unity of the Holy Spirit, world without end.

Coronation Service

Almighty God, the fountain of all goodness, we humbly beseech thee to bless our most gracious Sovereign Lady, Queen Elizabeth, and all the Royal Family: endue them with thy Holy Spirit; enrich them with thy heavenly grace; prosper them with all happiness; and bring them to thine everlasting kingdom; through Jesus Christ our Lord.

Prayer Book, 1662

❧

SCHOOL

Almighty God, in whom we live and move and have our being: make this school as a field which the Lord has blessed; that whatsoever things are true and pure, lovely and of good report, may here flourish and abound. Preserve in it an unblemished name, enlarge it to a wider usefulness, and exalt it in the love of all its members as an instrument of thy glory; through Jesus Christ our Lord.

King's School, Canterbury

SOCIETY, THE NATION AND THE WORLD

Into thy hands, O heavenly Father, I commit myself, body and soul. Let thy holy angel be with me, that the evil one may have no power over me. Help and bless thy church; hold thy protecting hand over this land and people; have pity upon those who are in distress and need. O God, let the light of thy truth shine upon us, and bring us at last to thy heavenly kingdom; through Jesus Christ our Lord.

Martin Luther

Merciful God, to thee we commend ourselves and all those who need thy help and correction. Where there is hatred, give love; where there is injury, pardon; where there is doubt, faith; where there is despair, hope; where there is sadness, joy; where there is darkness, light. Grant that we may seek not so much to be consoled, as to console; to be understood, as to understand; to be loved, as to love; for in giving we receive, in pardoning we are pardoned, and dying we are born into eternal life.

St. Francis

O Lord Jesus Christ, who was lifted upon the cross to draw all men unto thee, look in mercy, we beseech thee, upon this nation. Send out thy light and thy truth that they may lead us into the paths of fellowship and peace; break down all barriers of contention and strife; and grant that, seeking first thy kingdom and righteousness, we may live together in brotherly love and concord, to thy glory and the welfare of this realm. Hear us, blessed Lord, to whom, with the Father and the Holy Spirit, be all honour and glory, world without end.

Bishop Theodore Woods

Almighty God, from whom all thoughts of truth and peace proceed: kindle, we pray thee, in the hearts of all men the true love of peace; and guide with thy pure and peaceable wisdom those who take counsel for the nations of the world; that in tranquillity thy kingdom may go forward, till the earth is filled with the knowledge of thy love; through Jesus Christ our Lord.

Prayer Book, 1928

O God, who hast ordained that men should live and work together as brethren: remove, we humbly beseech thee, from those who are now at variance, all spirit of strife and all occasion of bitterness, that, seeking only what is just and equal, they may ever continue in brotherly union and concord, to their own well-being, and the prosperity of the realm; through Jesus Christ our Lord.

Prayer Book, 1928

THANKSGIVING

Almighty God, Father of all mercies, we thine unworthy servants do give thee most humble and hearty thanks for all thy goodness and loving kindness to us and to all men; we bless thee for our creation, preservation, and all the blessings of this life; but above all for thine inestimable love in the redemption of the world by our Lord Jesus Christ; for the means of grace, and for the hope of glory. And, we beseech thee, give us that due sense of all thy mercies, that our hearts may be unfeignedly thankful, and that we shew forth thy praise, not only with our lips, but in our lives; by giving up ourselves to thy service, and by walking before thee in holiness and righteousness all our days; through Jesus Christ our Lord, to whom with thee and the Holy Ghost be all honour and glory, world without end.

Prayer Book, 1662

For Ourselves

BIBLE

O Lord God, who hast left us thy holy Word to be a lantern unto our feet, and a light unto our steps: give unto us all thy Holy Spirit, that out of the same Word we may learn what is thy eternal will, and frame our lives in all obedience to the same, to thy honour and glory and the increase of our faith; through Jesus Christ our Lord.

Edward Dering

Blessed Lord, by whose providence all Holy Scriptures were written and preserved for our instruction: give us grace to study them each day with patience and love; strengthen our souls with the fulness of their divine teaching; keep from us all pride and irreverence; guide us in the deep things of thy heavenly wisdom; and, of thy great mercy, lead us by thy Word into everlasting life.

Bishop Westcott

Blessed Lord, who has caused all holy Scriptures to be written for our learning: grant that we may in such wise hear them, read, mark, learn and inwardly digest them, that by patience and comfort of thy holy Word, we may embrace and ever hold fast the blessed hope of everlasting life, which thou hast given us in our Saviour Jesus Christ.

Prayer Book, 1662

BLESSING

The blessing of the Lord rest and remain upon all his people, in every land, of every tongue; the Lord meet in mercy all that seek him; the Lord comfort all who suffer and mourn; the Lord hasten his coming, and give us, his people, peace by all means.

Bishop Handley Moule

To God the Father, who loved us, and made us accepted in the Beloved: to God the Son, who loved us and washed us from our sins in his own blood: to God the Holy Ghost, who sheds the love of God abroad in our hearts: be all love and glory for time and for eternity.

Bishop Thomas Ken

COMMITTAL

Into thy hands I commend my spirit, soul, body: thou hast created, redeemed, regenerated them, O Lord of truth, and with me all mine and all things mine: thou hast bestowed them upon me, O Lord, in thy goodness. Preserve us from all evil, preserve our souls, I beseech thee, O Lord: keep us from falling and present us faultless before thy presence in that day. Let the words of my mouth and the meditation of my heart be always acceptable in thy sight, O Lord, my rock and my redeemer.

Lancelot Andrewes

COURAGE

Heavenly Father, the Father of all wisdom, understanding, and true strength, we beseech thee to look mercifully upon thy servants, and send thy Holy Spirit into their hearts, that when they must join to fight in the field for the glory of thy holy name, then they, strengthened with the defence of thy right hand, may manfully stand in the confession of thy faith, and continue in the same unto their lives' end.

Bishop Nicholas Ridley

DEDICATION

O Lord, Jesus Christ, who hast created and redeemed me, and hast brought me unto that which now I am, thou knowest what thou wouldst do with me; do with me according to thy will; for thy tender mercy's sake.

King Henry VI

Lord, grant us grace, to make thy goodness our trust: shutting our hearts against pride, our mouths against evil words, our ears against foul knowledge, and using thy gifts to the promotion of thy glory and of man's salvation; for his blessed sake, in whom we have all and are full and abound, Jesus Christ.

Christina Rossetti

Send out thy light and thy truth, that I may live always near to thee, my God. Let me feel thy love, that I may be — as it were — already in heaven, that I may do my work as the angels do theirs; and let me be ready for every work, be ready to go out or to go in, to stay or depart, just as thou shalt appoint. Lord, let me have no will of my own, or consider my happiness as depending in the smallest degree on anything that can befall me outwardly, but as consisting altogether in conformity to thy will.

Henry Martyn

Take, Lord, all my liberty. Receive my memory, my understanding, and my whole will. Whatever I have and possess thou hast given to me; to thee I restore it wholly, and to thy will I utterly surrender it for thy direction. Give me the love of thee only, with thy grace, and I am rich enough; nor ask I anything beside.

Ignatius of Loyola

Use me, my Saviour, for whatever purpose and in whatever way thou mayest require. Here is my poor heart, an empty vessel: fill it with thy grace. Here is my sinful and troubled soul: quicken it and refresh it with thy love. Take my heart for thine abode; my mouth to spread abroad the glory of thy name; my love and all my powers for the advancement of thy believing people; and never suffer the steadfastness and confidence of my faith to abate.

Dwight L. Moody

Thanks be to thee, my Lord Jesus Christ, for all the benefits which thou hast given to me, for all the pains and insults which thou hast borne for me. O most merciful Redeemer, Friend, and Brother, may I know thee more clearly, love thee more dearly, and follow thee more nearly.

St. Richard of Chichester

Almighty and eternal God, so draw our hearts to thee, so guide our minds, so fill our imaginations, so control our wills, that we may be wholly thine, utterly dedicated to thee; and then use us, we pray thee, as thou wilt, but always to thy glory and the welfare of thy people, through our Lord and Saviour, Jesus Christ.

Archbishop William Temple

Oalmighty God, who alone canst order the unruly wills and affections of sinful men: grant unto thy people, that they may love the thing which thou commandest, and desire that which thou dost promise; that so, among the sundry and manifold changes of the world, our hearts may surely there be fixed where true joys are to be found; through Jesus Christ our Lord.

Prayer Book, 1662

FORGIVENESS

Most great and glorious Lord God, accept my imperfect repentance, and send thy Spirit of adoption into my heart, that I may again be owned by thee, call thee Father, and share in the blessings of thy children.

John Wesley

Almighty Father, Lord of heaven and earth, we confess that we have sinned against thee in thought, word and deed. Have mercy upon us, O Lord, have mercy upon us after thy great goodness; according to the multitude of thy mercies, do away our offences: wash us throughly from our wickedness, and cleanse us from our sins; for Jesus Christ's sake.

Canadian Prayer Book

Lord, of thy great goodness I beseech thee give me true repentance, and forgive me all my sins, negligences and ignorances, and endue me with the grace of thy Holy Spirit, that I may amend my life according to thy holy word.

Archbishop Laud

Grant, we beseech thee, merciful Lord, to thy faithful people pardon and peace; that they may be cleansed from all their sins, and serve thee with a quiet mind; through Jesus Christ our Lord.

Prayer Book, 1662

Almighty and everlasting God, who art always more ready to hear that we to pray, and art wont to give more than either we desire or deserve: pour down upon us the abundance of thy mercy; forgiving us those things whereof our conscience is afraid, and giving us those good things which we are not worthy to ask, but through the merits and mediation of Jesus Christ, the Son, our Lord.

Prayer Book, 1662

GUIDANCE

O God, by whom the meek are guided in judgement, and light riseth up in darkness for the godly: grant us in all our doubts and uncertainties, the grace to ask what thou wouldst have us to do; that the Spirit of wisdom may save us from all false choices, and that in thy light we may see light and in thy straight path may not stumble; through Jesus Christ our Lord.

William Bright

Make us of quick and tender conscience, O Lord; that understanding we may obey every word of thine, and discerning may follow every suggestion of thine indwelling Spirit. Speak, Lord, for thy servant heareth.

Christina Rossetti

Lord, we pray thee that thy grace may always prevent and follow us, and make us continually to be given to all good works; through Jesus Christ our Lord.

Prayer Book, 1662

Grant to us, Lord, we beseech thee, the spirit to think and do always such things as be rightful; that we, who cannot do anything that is good without thee, may by thee be enabled to live according to thy will; through Jesus Christ our Lord.

Prayer Book, 1662

God grant me the serenity to accept the things I cannot change; the courage to change the things I can; and the wisdom to know the difference.

Rienholdt Niebuhr

❧

HOLY SPIRIT

O heavenly Father, the author and fountain of all truth, send, we beseech thee, thy Holy Spirit into our hearts, and enlighten our understandings with the beams of thy heavenly grace. We ask this, O merciful Father, for thy dear Son, our Saviour, Jesus Christ's sake.

Bishop Nicholas Ridley

O God, forasmuch as without thee we are not able to please thee; mercifully grant, that thy Holy Spirit may in all things direct and rule our hearts; through Jesus Christ our Lord.

Prayer Book, 1662

Almighty God, unto whom all hearts be open, all desires known, and from whom no secrets are hid: cleanse the thoughts of our hearts by the inspiration of thy Holy Spirit, that we may perfectly love thee, and worthily magnify thy holy name; through Jesus Christ our Lord.

Prayer Book, 1662

❧

HUMILITY

O Lord Jesus Christ, who didst humble thyself to become man, and to be born into the world for our salvation: teach us the grace of humility, root out of our hearts all pride and haughtiness, and so fashion us after thy holy likeness, that in the world to come we may be made like unto thee; for thine own name's and mercies' sake.

Bishop Walsham How

O Lord Jesus Christ, who for our sakes didst leave the light and glory of thy Father's presence, came and dwelt amongst us in poverty, and suffered death upon a cross of shame; let this mind also be in us, that we may not seek great things for ourselves, but follow in the steps of thy humility, for thy name's sake.

Anon.

༄

KNOWLEDGE OF GOD

Almighty God, give us wisdom to perceive thee, intellect to understand thee, diligence to seek thee, patience to wait for thee, vision to behold thee, a heart to meditate upon thee, and life to proclaim thee.

St. Benedict

༄

LIFE AFTER DEATH

O heavenly Father, who in thy Son Jesus Christ, hast given us a true faith, and a sure hope; help us, we pray thee, to live as those who believe and trust in the communion of saints, the forgiveness of sins, and the resurrection to life everlasting, and strengthen this faith and hope in us all the days of our life: through the love of thy Son, Jesus Christ our Saviour.

Prayer Book, 1928

༄

LIKENESS TO CHRIST

O God, who before the passion of thine only-begotten Son didst reveal his glory upon the holy mount; grant unto us thy servants, that in faith beholding the light of his countenance, we may be strengthened to bear the cross, and be changed into his likeness from glory to glory; through the same Jesus Christ our Lord.

Prayer Book, 1928

LOVE

Grant us grace, O Father, not to pass by suffering or joy without eyes to see; give us understanding and sympathy, and guard us from selfishness, that we may enter into the joys and sufferings of others; use us to gladden and strengthen those who are weak and suffering; that by our lives we may help others to believe and serve thee, and shed forth thy light which is the light of life.

H. R. L. Sheppard

O Lord, who hast taught us that all our doings without charity are nothing worth: send thy Holy Ghost, and pour into our hearts that most excellent gift of charity, the very bond of peace and of all virtues, without which whosoever liveth is counted dead before thee; grant this for thine only Son Jesus Christ's sake.

Prayer Book, 1662

O God, who hast prepared for them that love thee such good things as pass man's understanding: pour into our hearts such love toward thee, that we, loving thee above all things, may obtain thy promises, which exceed all that we can desire; through Jesus Christ our Lord.

Prayer Book, 1662

OBEDIENCE

Deliver me, O God, from a slothful mind, from all lukewarmness, and all dejection of spirit. I know these cannot but deaden my love to thee; mercifully free my heart from them, and give me a lively, zealous, active, and cheerful spirit; that I may vigorously perform whatever thou commandest, thankfully suffer whatever thou choosest for me, and be ever ardent to obey in all things thy holy love.

John Wesley

PRAISE

O God, who requirest that we should seek thee and makest us to find thee, and openest to us when we knock: O God from whom to be averted is to fall, and to whom to be turned is to rise; in whom to abide is to be established; O God, whom to know is to live, whom to serve is to reign; I praise thee, I bless thee, I adore thee, my God.

St. Augustine

Thine, O Lord, is the greatness, and the power, and the glory, and the victory, and the majesty: for all that is in heaven and in the earth is thine; thine is the kingdom, O Lord, and thou art exalted as head above all. Both riches and honour come of thee, and thou rulest over all; and in thine hand is power and might; and in thine hand it is to make great, and to give strength unto all. Now therefore, our God, we thank thee, and praise thy glorious name.

1 Chronicles 29:11 - 13

O thou, in whom all things live, who commandest us to seek thee and art ready to be found; to know thee is life, to serve thee is freedom, to praise thee is our souls' joy. We bless thee and adore thee, we worship thee and glorify thee, we give thanks to thee for thy great glory. Maker and preserver of all things visible and invisible, keep, we beseech thee, the work of thine own hands, now and at all times; through Jesus Christ our Lord.

St. Augustine

PRAYER

O almighty God, from whom every good prayer cometh, and who pourest out on all who desire it the spirit of grace and supplication: deliver us, when we draw nigh to thee, from coldness of heart and wanderings of mind, that with steadfast thoughts and kindled affections we may worship thee in spirit and in truth; through Jesus Christ our Lord.

William Bright

SERVICE

Teach us, good Lord, to serve thee as thou deservest; to give and not to count the cost; to fight and not to heed the wounds; to toil and not to seek for rest; to labour and not to ask for any reward, save that of knowing that we do thy will; through Jesus Christ our Lord.

Ignatius of Loyola

Stir up, we beseech thee, O Lord, the wills of thy faithful people, that they, plenteously bringing forth the fruit of good works, may of thee be plenteously rewarded; through Jesus Christ our Lord.

Prayer Book, 1662

O Lord Jesus Christ, whose service is perfect freedom, shew us what we can do for thee; give us the strength to do it with all our hearts; and help us to give thee all the glory; for the sake of thy holy name.

Anon.

O God, when thou givest to thy servants to endeavour in any great matter, help us to know that it is not the beginning, but the continuing of the same until it be thoroughly finished that yieldeth the true glory; through Jesus Christ our Lord.

After Sir Francis Drake

STRENGTH

Be, Lord, within me to strengthen me, without me to preserve, over me to shelter, beneath me to support, before me to direct, behind me to bring back, round me to fortify.

Lancelot Andrewes

TEMPTATION, TROUBLE, etc.

O God, who knowest us to be set in the midst of so many and great dangers, that by season of the failty of our nature we cannot always stand upright: grant us such strength and protection, as may support us in all dangers and carry us through all temptations; through Jesus Christ our Lord.

Prayer Book, 1662

O Lord God, who seest that we put not our trust in anything that we do: mercifully grant that by thy power we may be defended against all adversity; through Jesus Christ our Lord.

Prayer Book, 1662

Almighty God, who seest that we have no power of ourselves to help ourselves: keep us both outwardly in our bodies, and inwardly in our souls; that we may be defended from all adversities which may happen to the body, and from all evil thoughts which may assault and hurt the soul; through Jesus Christ our Lord.

Prayer Book, 1662

Grant, O Lord, that these anxious and perplexing days may be lived in the calm of thy presence, in the enjoyment of thy peace, in the experience of thy power, and in the obedience of thy will. Guide us in difficulty, protect us in danger, guard us in temptation; that in thought, word and deed we may live to bring honour and pleasure to thy holy name; through Jesus Christ, our Lord.

Anon.

Lord, we beseech thee, grant thy people grace to withstand the temptations of the world, the flesh, and the devil, and with pure hearts and minds to follow thee the only God; through Jesus Christ our Lord.

Prayer Book, 1662

A Personal Litany

'SORRY'

From entertaining thoughts that are proud, impure or selfish; from forgetting you in the rush of daily life; and from failing to consider the needs and wishes of my family and my friends.

Deliver me, O Lord.

From showing contempt for those who are less fortunate or successful than I, and from envy and jealousy of those who are more so; from impatience and intolerance towards those with whom I disagree; and from feeling bitter and resentful towards those who seem to have treated me with injustice, suspicion, envy or malice.

Deliver me, O Lord.

From speaking carelessly, spitefully and untruthfully; from a desire always to be right and a reluctance to apologise; from a determination at any cost to win a game or an argument, and from being sulky and ungenerous in defeat.

Deliver me, O Lord.

From being a hypocrite in order to make a good impression or to curry favour; from sacrificing principle for popularity; from forsaking duty for pleasure, or the hard right for the easy wrong; from shrinking through fear from some difficult choice or demanding challenge; and from being ashamed to be known as a Christian.

Deliver me, O Lord.

'THANKS'

For your constant and steadfast kindness and care; for food and health and shelter; for the fact that all things work together for good to those who love you; and that nothing can hurt or harm me without your permission.

I thank you, O Lord.

For the love of parents and children, and the companionship of relations and friends; for the challenge of work and games, and for all my powers of mind and body; for all that is beautiful, and good, and true in nature, in music, in art and literature, and in the lives of men and women.

I thank you, O Lord.

For the measureless gift of your Son, Jesus Christ; for the example he set, the teaching he gave, the miracles he performed; for his death upon the cross as my Saviour and Redeemer; and for his glorious resurrection and ascension.

I thank you, O Lord.

For the provision you have made for my steady growth as a Christian; for the Bible and prayer, for my church and Christian friends, for the freedom to worship you in peace, for all the means of grace and for the hope of glory.

I thank you, O Lord.

'PLEASE'

That you will bless our country — the Queen and the Royal Family, the leaders in church and state, industry and the services, and all its citizens everywhere; that your Spirit, shed abroad in the hearts of your people, may drive from its shores injustice, cruelty, poverty and enmity between different classes and races; and that we may all learn to live together as one family in peace and good will.

Lord, in your mercy hear my prayer.

That you will look with compassion upon all who are in any way afflicted or distressed: upon all prisoners and captives; upon the victims of flood or famine, persecution or war; and upon all who suffer, or mourn the loss of those whom they love; and that you will guide and strengthen doctors, nurses, clergy and all those who seek to bring help and comfort where there is sickness and sorrow.

Lord, in your mercy hear my prayer.

That I may play my full part in the life of my home, my school, my daily business and my church; that my presence in all these may be an example, an encouragement and even an inspiration to others; and that as far as possible I may learn to live in love and peace with all men, and even with those whom I find it hard to like.

Lord, in your mercy hear my prayer.

That day by day I may grow more like you, until others can see in me a reflection of your love and joy, and may begin to feel after you and to find you for themselves; and that I may never be ashamed to confess the faith of Christ crucified, but manfully to fight under his banner against sin, the world and the devil.

Lord, in your mercy hear my prayer.